THE LEGEND OF MICHAEL JACKSON

THE LEGEND OF MICHAEL JACKSON

TRISTAN EVERGREEN

CONTENTS

CHAPTER 1

Introduction

An influential, entertaining, and unrivaled star, Michael Jackson had amassed devoted followers who remained connected to his music and amiable conduct. He continued to support underlying motives, such as philanthropy and social service. His supporters would remember his devotion to music. Every person in his Miscellanies Discourses particularly and specifically every piece, every one, and every bit reveals his unforeseen potential and judgment. He not only transformed his songs through his sensual feel and touch and painted Eden by the power of his voice, but he also diverted American music in an entirely new and diverse direction.

The name 'Michael Jackson' is a name that is familiar to a lot of people, old and young. His name continues to be recognized by those in diverse clans and tribes. When his name is called during celebrity news or documentaries, there seems to be an invisible spark that passes through their hearts, causing them to feel his presence, or spread a smile or a feeling of longing. He exudes so much musical spirituality and impact that no matter how long he's been gone, he'll eternally dwell in their hearts. In this article, we'll learn more about Michael Jackson's life and legacy all the way from his death to his sacred divinity. Here, we're entering a world that seeks to hold forth some of Michael Jackson's lovely and loyal followers, his fame, his music, how his genre promoted a new age of music in the United States, and a lot more through the conclusions of this paper.

Background and Context

Serving time as a moderate hard-worker, Michael Jackson spent almost his whole life on the road and in the recording studio. There was no time for the man behind the music to put his feet up as he was often becoming increasingly famous and wanted as an entertainer. This research paper will focus attention on this extraordinary man as a person and the world of music in which such talent was fostered and squeezed out. Michael Joseph Jackson was born on Friday, August 29th, 1958, in Gary, Indiana, USA. Originally entitled "Joseph," Michael Joseph was renamed shortly after by his parents, Katherine and Joseph Jackson. Michael was the seventh of nine children. Since the release in 1982 of the blueprint album "Thriller," Michael Jackson emerged as a definitive 20th-century performer, the single figure that embodied the times in which he lived. He was also one of the most critically celebrated and commercially successful pop artists in American music history.

His life was unusual. He transcended R&B and broke down the different "color lines" in African American-inspired music, providing a way for MTV to be broadcast to a white audience. As a singer and dancer, he was easily one of the most popular performers to cheer us up with the sweet sound of his music. The nuances of his life not only affected the way he made it easier but also influenced many people after him, making his music a force to be reckoned with. He was America, despite some of the nation's denials, a former slave owner, who also had a subliminal attraction with African American culture. In the middle of this pulse lay Michael Jackson, a singer and dancer who stepped onto the scene of American pop culture in 1969 as the unmarried lead singer of the bubblegum soul band the Jackson 5 and moved on to his own superstardom in the 1970s.

CHAPTER 2

Early Life and Career

Michael's childhood underscored core themes in his work: power and morality, sacrifice and redemption, transformation and transcendence, choice and vision. And, as with his music, Michael didn't simply live these archetypal experiences; he turned them into universal stories. This capability would prove his biggest gift to humankind.

The boy who would become Michael Jackson was born on August 29, 1958, one of ten children living on a tidy street in Gary, Indiana, a blue-collar town forty minutes from the heart of Chicago. Brought up in a two-room house with his older sisters, Rebbie, La-Toya, and Janet, he was called Mikey by those dearest to him - Ma, Pa, and his siblings.

As a little boy, he was a dancing marvel. If his feet were still, his head bopped to an inner rhythm too complex to fully express, so he moved his entire body to the beat. Passed down from his father, Joseph - a crane operator for the local steel mill - the gift of grace underlined Mikey's budding career as a singer and one day as the King of Pop. Since he displayed none of Tito's fickleness, his older brothers were more careful nurturing Mikey. Randy, who watched after Mikey like a second father, also spied him. Even more important than his relations with his brothers, however, was his mother's influence. A deeply spiritual woman, Katherine Jackson instilled in her children the virtues of moral living and the humble acceptance of God's will. Such values, crucial elements in Michael's art, only led to what would dominate his life.

Childhood and Family

Michael Joseph Jackson (August 29, 1958 - June 25, 2009) is the King of Pop. He is an American singer, dancer, songwriter, and performer. Jackson has had a profound influence on the world of music and dance. His contribution to music, dance, and fashion is recognized by music critics. He has brought music to a completely new level and has played an important role in the development of a variety of music forms. His music video has influenced contemporary music videos in form and content, bringing the potential of music videos as a promotional and marketing tool to new heights and setting the precedent for future music videos. His album Thriller is the most successful album of his period, with record sales of over 100 million worldwide, according to the Guinness World Records, and one of the best-selling music albums of all time.

Michael Jackson, the eighth of ten children in the Jackson family, grew up in a rural family with a love of music. His father, Joseph Jackson, is a steel plant employee. His mother, Catherine Jackson, is a housewife. From childhood, Katherine's family's nine children formed a singing and dancing group called the Jackson Journey. The talented Michael Jackson, who joined the Jackson Journey in 1964, could sing and dance in a superior way at a very young age. He was the lead singer of the group in his teenage years. In 1971, Michael Jackson began his solo career with the release of "Got to Be There." Despite still being a member of the Jackson Journey, in 1979, Jackson met with the director. During his height, he had undergone significant plastic surgery in a period of time, and his appearance had undergone a significant change.

The Jackson 5

The Jacksons remained fairly constant in their early years, consisting of the five brothers. Tito, the oldest, played the guitar and was the lead singer. Marlon, the second oldest, also played guitar and was a lead singer with Tito. Jackie, the third oldest, played drums if and when there was a formal accompanist group, and sang solo with them. Michael, the fourth oldest, was the lead singer, playing the conga and tambourine when one was available. Jermaine, the youngest, played the bass guitar and sang solo. When an acoustic guitar was desired in the band, Jermaine would play that while Tito went back to the bongos.

The Jackson boys began singing and dancing for pleasure during their rough-and-tumble West Side Chicago youth. As a result of that activity, they picked up a variety of show business engagements in the city. Their mother drove them back and forth when the group wanted her to. They were performing at the local YMCA when they got their break. Gladys Knight, the singing star and head of her own highly popular female group, was performing at the YMCA, and at the urging of her father, took a look and a listen to the Jacksons. She was impressed with the five boys and thought twice when she heard their rendition of her number one song, "Some Day We'll Be Together," a hit song. She called the founder of the famous Motown record company, Barry Gordy, and to make a long story short, he immediately called Chicago and told the Jacksons if they would try a hit number for him, he would fly to Chicago, listen to it, and might sign them to a recording contract. They tried the song and Mr. Gordy went to Chicago. He signed a contract with the leading Chicago singing group on the spot after hearing them perform the hit record. The Jackson 5 (soon to become the most sensational boy singing group in show business and earn the title of "The Rolling Stones of the Seventies") was on their way to stardom at an early age.

CHAPTER 3

Breakthrough as a Solo Artist

After the victory of West End musical Thriller Live in a case brought by Michael Jackson's estate for using the copyrighted image of the late performer, the show has lost a bid to have the appeal against the verdict in the Court of Appeal dismissed. Having been together for nearly a decade, Jackson Five went their separate ways in 1984, after which Michael Jackson embarked on what was to be an ultra-successful solo journey. Jackson, 24 at this point, had been preparing to go solo for several years, and was working with the likes of Quincy Jones in order to make this transition as seamless as possible. He had also signed a licensing deal with Epic Records, and released his first album as an adult in 1979. Entitled Off The Wall, Jackson's fourth release ended up becoming the first album to have four singles with Billboard Hot 100 chart successes. It sold twenty million copies worldwide and was awarded a Grammy for Album of the Year, as well as Best Male R&B Vocal Performance thanks to Don't Stop 'Til You Get Enough.

The release of Thriller three years later would go on to define Jackson's status as an international superstar, as well as garner considerable attention in the music industry. "Thriller has become the biggest selling album in history," Rolling Stone's celebrated critic Vincent Canby wrote in 1983. "It's one of the few recordings in any field that attracts the indiscriminate enthusiasm of nonamateur fans and nonapproving critics alike. It is liked even by those who supposedly dislike it when the occasion arises." With sales surpassing 70 million, Thriller has turned out to be one of the most critically acclaimed albums in history and Jackson's highest-selling recording. True to form, the list of awards it has received over the years is staggering, including Victoires de la Musique, the London Critics Circles Award, the Guinness World Records, and an induction into the Grammy Hall of Fame.

Off the Wall

After three years of non-stop touring, Michael sneaked into the recording studios and laid down tracks which would eventually become his fifth album, Off the Wall. Initial sales were slow in a music market where playlists for black music were already crawling scratchily out of old black & white TV sets care of Juke Box Jury. The first million flowed from racks to racks more slowly than expected. Things started turning around early in 1980, the record started breaking through. An interesting point to note is that Off the Wall was not and is not a 'best seller'. Like everything, Michael bought resources time for his fans.

However, Off the Wall remains one of the biggest-selling albums in modern music. It's just that they never managed to catch the numbers of its successor, Thriller. It still turned big enough to be one of the biggest-selling albums in history. In America, Off the Wall battled the rock and roll the disco of the Bee Gees and the lycanthigail obsessions of Joe Jackson and his herd. But even in post-disco, organ-grinding America, it turned Michael out a hatful of top 10 hits. Most important, it fixated in record company managers' minds, producers' minds, and MTV executives' minds, the belief that Michael was a "cross-over" artist with potential for earning money off as a solo. Right in the middle of being invited to join Al Green on the keyboard, Michael released a record, Off the Wall. Off the Wall was romantic, pulsating music drawing on disco music like the mirror ball in Studio 54, also featured a repertoire of ballads neatly dished to the other sexes.

Thriller

Michael Jackson had begun writing songs for his next album, using synthesizers and digital sound. Released in November 1982, Thriller cost more than $700,000 to create. CBS said it would consider "a modest profit" to be selling a mere 250,000 copies. Thriller was at Number One before Christmas. 4 billion sales later, the album has become the best-selling album of all time and has seen off competition from millions of others. It spent 19 weeks at number one, set a new standard: seven of the ten tracks were released, and every one made the Top 10. An astonishing 39 million copies have been sold. As well as being awarded a then record of 8 Grammy awards, more than any album had ever won, Thriller won countless other awards, including album of the year.

The album won Michael a new and legion of fans in every demographic, from metal heads to rock criticisms and from infant in the cradle. Everybody, from the family audience to hard-core funk fans, adored Thriller. It was the album that everybody seemed to have en all the major star, from Prince to George Michael, had sent me written message of congratulation. Michael had the star quality, the success, by far and away the biggest he had ever had in his long, successful career, came at a time when it meant the most to him. This was Michael Jackson's breakthrough. He was now a superstar, on a global scale. Michael was a megastar. Michael was the King of Pop.

CHAPTER 4

Innovations and Influence

Apart from the hundreds of millions of records he sold, the one billion dollars he generated through music, and his status as a global sex symbol for the last four decades of his life, Michael Jackson attracted attention for the way in which he revolutionized the industry which broke him into prominence. From the moment "Thriller" - still the highest-selling album of all time - was released 40 years ago, Jackson attracted millions of additional fans through achievements unconnected to his music. Certainly, the political painter Bob Dylan was a protest singer enshrining political and social issues into music which he later won the Nobel Prize for; and Eminem became one for his drug-, ex-wife-, and mother-abusing lyrics. But the tales Jackson told of white racism, capitalism gone awry, and personal isolation were fundamentally apolitical. His innovations, including a canonical music video, were in the artistic realm. Soon, his career became inextricably linked with dance, which is how he hid pain.

Not only his music but songs by his siblings, and their variety show, were heavily influenced by iconic African-American performers such as Little Richard and James Brown. But only Michael beat

Elvis and Stevie Wonder, then outperformed Madonna, of Italian descent, and contemporarily outperformed fellow African-American competitors, in global sales, radio rotations, Grammy Awards, and promotion by MTV. He was arguably the first celebrity who conclusively embodied white America's idea of an African-American, both the good and the bad. Talk of crossover was specious: He was inferential cross-cultural. If he invented nothing in music and dance, where does that leave Little Richard and James Brown? Michael was not post-Black but the paragon of the Black Arts Movement. Predictably, after he died, popular music in the US failed to produce as many knockouts befitting one of his concerts; it is difficult to imagine his own afterlife overarching pop a mass production.

Music Videos

Music videos: Michael Jackson transformed the landscape of music videos. Production expenditures on music videos increased as channels searched for new music and alternative ways to market artists. MTV and VH1 played a significant role in exposing Jackson to a vast number of new potential fans. This visual framing of sound enabled viewers throughout the world to dance and sing along to a song that would leave a lasting impression. Some of Jackson's most iconic videos, such as "Beat It," "Thriller," "Billie Jean," "Smooth Criminal," and "Bad," used imagery combined with storytelling to entice and excite a worldwide audience.

Jackson's work is the turning point for the music video industry, stating, "Jackson made music videos viable as a product, not just a tool for promotion."

Eos: Beautifully choreographed, Jackson took up to thirty-one hours to complete the special effects work needed to turn Jackson into a werewolf, his dancers into zombies, and to film the final thriller dance. Studios: Jackson used traditional stages like Tatino

Brothers, United Studios, and Capitol Records, as well as non-traditional stages like underground subways and city streets. Jackson also started his own production company, MJJ Productions. In addition to traditional stages, Jackson's videos from "Scream" to "Hollywood Tonight" also used film studios such as Los Angeles Center Studios, Sepulveda Dam Basin, and Orpheum Theater. Movement: Jackson infuses passion and storytelling into his movements. From the "attempted walking" in "Billie Jean" to the wild and pulsing dance in "Smooth Criminal" to the "fierce" meeting "Bad," Jackson's sharp, precise, and fluid movements are the defining influence on his art. Iconic: Beyond their stunning visual effects, these decades-old videos have stood the test of time. In the 1980s, Vogue dubbed "Thriller" "the most successful music video in history," and VH1 declared it a "visual watershed." In 2009, "Thriller" was entered into the National Film Registry as "culturally, historically, or aesthetically" significant by the Library of Congress.

Dance Moves

With their mesmerizing, hook-filled songs, the Jackson 5 were already a sensation, but it wasn't until the younger Jackson stepped out onto a wide, glittering stage of coaxial-cable-connected television screens that pop culture would never be the same. In a loose, rhinestoned military jacket designed by his mother and utilizing a patented dance move as old as minstrelsy, Michael Jackson moonwalked his way into history on a May 16, 1983, broadcast of the Motown 25: Yesterday, Today and Forever special.

Jackson himself had actually debuted the moonwalk earlier, performing the dance step on short music films airing during commercials. But this prime-time appearance before an estimated audience of 47 million brought the jittery EVA triumph to the masses. It resonated culturally and would show up everywhere from high-school talent shows to breakdancing craze parties, inspiring the adorning of many a pair of old penny loafers with slippery socks. Jackson's crisp performances have always included much dancing, surely, and before these, plenty of similarly influenced steps in his videos," critic Margo Jefferson wrote in her New York Times review of Jackson's "Bad." In that, he was something altogether new: a song-and-dance man whose meandering moves told you about the meaning of the music. Michael Jackson came up during a post-Civil Rights era of television variety shows and a burgeoning music video industry. He knew how to work onscreen, as a singer, an actor, and a dancer. His videos and TV performances allowed him to give us a visual storyline on top of the music, and gave him free rein to use the camera like a magnifying glass. In recognizing his ability to innervate, to inject feeling and metaphor into every moment of a song (its near-decadent perfectionism), we recognize that, in reality, these endlessly watchable videos encapsulate Michael Jackson's artistry better than any other performances, on the big screen or small. He was truly a man of the age of cable television. He was a storyteller who, with his tight moves and signature lean, could churn out minute-long moods that lingered in a listener's memory bank like hit radio. And the moves Jackson made in his telling of that story were as indelible as his music. From his swinging shoulders and swiveling head to the white glitter glove of his moonwalk debut to the kick and dribble of "Billy Jean" and the infectious jete of "Beat It," his performances were equally dance and theater. "On the music video screen, Michael Jackson's dancing has never been more inviting, spunky, and spontaneous," Jefferson wrote. And at a time when programs like Soul Train and the Pat B. Harrison-hosted series Superstars of the Black Dance showcased the best of funk and hustle, "It was the insouciance of the moods that communicated. And so the dancing communicated most, as Jackson's body sang along with him." It still does. "Innovative choreography with cutting-edge effects, signature dance moves, plus an exceptional performance by guest guitarist Ed Daly (e.g. his spider-like presence on the screen) bring a flashback of vintage pop culture," one viewer wrote of the Millennium Party video. "One of the very best." "Every time I see it I learn a new MJ move," wrote another. "Michael was truly the best," commented yet another. "So many seemed to miss out on how he truly incorporated every move with the music."

CHAPTER 5

Challenges and Controversies

Problems often arise where talent is involved. Whether through whispers or outright disdain or rivalry, Michael Jackson often faced ceaseless criticism and skepticism. As he inched his way into adulthood, much of the scrutiny landed on the endearing pop star known for "Thriller" and his gravity-defying moonwalk. As much as Michael transcended, he also faced downhill spirals that would haunt him all the way to his premature demise in June of 2009. Challenges did arise in the mid-1980s only to morph into more sinister controversies in the 1990s.

In May of 1984, Michael was conducting the last show in his North American Victory Tour when he was stricken with pneumonia. He had been taking prescribed painkillers ever since severely burning his scalp on the set of a Pepsi commercial. The addiction saved off a media frenzy until February of 1986, when he was diagnosed with vitiligo, a disease where an individual loses melanin on certain parts of their body. Although evidence suggested otherwise due to his blemished autopsy, Michael insisted that he could not help that his skin turned progressively lighter. Plucked from his comfort zone in February of 1993, Michael was publicly accused of sexual abuse by Evan Chandler, a Beverly Hills dentist who was disgruntled after Michael broke off all contact with him. The jury eventually ruled in Michael's favor, dismissing the sexual abuse claims put forth by Jackson's family during a civil hearing. "People were not making this connection, and it caused me a lot of reluctance on my part," explains Michael. "When I saw that no one was drawing that parallel, I thought I needed to write a song about AIDS. I started writing 'We Are The World' that very night." During the week, Michael collaborated with Lionel Richie.

Legal Issues

A series of accusations were made against Michael Jackson during his life and beyond. In 1993, it became public that Michael Jackson was under investigation for molesting a child. The Chandlers, a family with whom Jackson became friends, filed a lawsuit against the pop singer, asking for $20 million to settle out of court. After investigation by the police, the District Attorney in Los Angeles closed the case stating that he could not prove Jackson's guilt. The family of the accuser continued with their lawsuit, eventually settling for an or so-called out-of-court settlement of about $24 million in January 1994. From the following years until 2003, there were no additional accusations made against Jackson.

Michael Jackson became entangled in a legal battle. In 2005, during the trial against him in Santa Maria, Jackson was accused by Gavin Arvizo. The accuser and his family stated having been held captive at Neverland Ranch and that Jackson had invited all of them to his tame, adult-night shows at Neverland. The family left Jake Alvaro, currently married to the accuser's sister, not married to him at the time of the trial, but a grownups mother and relatives. These people did not report wrongdoing to proper authorities but sought the assistance of a civil lawyer and, as a result, began hiring and firing criminal lawyers in swift succession. This trial could be discussed for its bizarre and extraordinary legal aspects. The additional charges are not what made this trial so remarkable; rather, it was the legal issues that were unusually striking, complex, and difficult.

Media Scrutiny

Michael Jackson was one of the media's favourite celebrities, and hundreds of news pieces were published or broadcast about him, especially during his more controversial moments and after his untimely death. The public's perception of Jackson was constantly changing, with the media playing a major part in these shifts. As noted by scholars interested in media representation of Jackson, the negative issues reported on, such as his molestation allegations, baby dangling incident, plastic surgeries, his 'whiter' skin and changing facial appearance, his strange or eccentric behaviour, and so on, received much more media play than his positive philanthropy, charity, and humanitarian works. These negative stories were featured far more and garnished massive headlines. Rumours that were surfacing about him were popular topics of discourse in major global news publications for months if not years, and his passing was a significant event reported on worldwide and was on the cover of most if not all major global newspapers.

As we have argued, as much media hype as Jackson got, the public cared less about Michael Jackson as a person and more about the mediated image of a global superstar. At the mere mention of his name, a wide array of comments and opinions, some stark and biased, were disseminated, and the public often paradoxically hated Jackson while at the same time loved and adored him. Despite the public's scrutiny and sensationalised stories, the media frenzy generated from those closely related issues also helped Jackson to become a more notorious public figure whose current impact and revenue has and will outlive his career as a performer.

CHAPTER 6

Philanthropy and Humanitarian Work

Michael Jackson was a vigorous advocate for numerous charitable causes. He founded the "Heal the World Foundation," along with his support for an estimated 39 charities and reportedly had global contributions of various forms exceeding $400 million. He also donated thousands of concert tickets for disadvantaged children worldwide and also set up drug rehabilitation centers both in the US and Europe. Jackson also supported many other charities, including the 46664 charity started by Nelson Mandela. These charities continue to be the recipients of Jackson's charitable support, long after his death. Soon after he was cleared of all sex offense charges, he was spotted in Bahrain, the Middle East country.

The first international event to be held at the Bahrain International Circuit, the Michael Jackson Tribute Concert, took place on 15 December 2007. This spectacular event abroad was dedicated to a humanitarian cause: to pay tribute to the late Michael Jackson and to support disadvantaged children worldwide. The international tribute was endorsed by Michael Jackson's mother, Katherine Jackson, who has given her blessing to the show. "We are delighted and honored to have Mrs. Jackson's support for our concert," commented Ron Nessim of Valor Music. Ticket sales included a charitable donation to UNESCO to support education for underprivileged children in developing nations. Michael Jackson was said to have been very pleased to do something that would benefit the less well off.

Charitable Contributions
Charitable Contributions (1988, 1995, 2006, 2009)

Michael Jackson continually donated and participated in various charitable activities and events. Listed here are a few examples of his donations and charitable activities.

According to The Guinness Book of World Records, The Michael Jackson Charitable Foundation broke a record. "Jackson has donated over $175 million in support of 39 charity organizations and has completed a reported 17-39 missions to help children worldwide" and in just one year (2000) broke his fundraising record at an event held for the foundation with a single-day donation amount totaling the One Million Dollar mark. He made contributions to The Make-A-Wish Foundation, UNICEF, The United Negro College Fund, Action Against Hunger/Friends of Congo/United Nation World Park, AIDS Project L.A, Project Angel Food, World Education, YMCA - 28th street/Crenshaw, Caring for Babies with AIDS, Chandler Lodge/Leo Buscaglia Foundation, The Los Angeles Children's Museum, United Friends of the Children and many more all over the world.

Final charities that got benefited from Michael are Children International, Ville de Refugie (City of Refuge), United Negro College, The Prince's Trust, The Rainbow Children's Development, Make-A-Wish Foundation, Mattel Children's Hospital, Love Match, UNICEF, Upward Bound House, Starlight Children's Foundation, The Macaulay Foundation, CaulW. Ban, A. Lock,

Turn Another Paige, The Waytech Group, The Hunger Project, Lola Children's Fund, Inc. Operating Engineers Local #12, Mentari USA, Juvenile Diabetes Research, Inner-City Games Foundation, H.E.L.P., Guardians of the Children, E.P.I.C., Dish 4 Kids, Diaspora International Tehed for Asmorestan Corporation, Common Threads, Calvert Social Investment Foundation, Camp & Campus, Beyond Zero Campaign, A-Place Called Home, The Abdul Rahim Ali Family Humanitarian Organization. Michael also gave $4,000.00 every month in the '60s till his death to the family of one of his best friends when they fell on hard times. Many children all over the world with broken bodies and spirits because of Hurricane Katrina only to name a few aesthetic works of love.

CHAPTER 7

Final Years and Death

Despite the negative press surrounding the last years of his life, Michael Jackson was a revered figure in entertainment, loved by countless millions of fans around the world spanning four decades. Besides winning hundreds of awards, including 13 Grammys, numerous American Music Awards and even the Bambi as well as Grammy Lifetime Achievement Awards, Jackson was one of the few artists who performed before the Pope and Queen. However, he lost his iconic status in part due to his extreme short-sightedness and his use of huge amounts of painkillers in a bid to silence the hounds of depression and the voices of those who wanted to enrich themselves at his expense.

Of the 500 million dollars he was due to raise for the July 2009 concerts, only 22 million dollars had been spent by him then. His serious uncompleted business and concert plans never came to fruition, as death called on him suddenly on Thursday, June 25, 2009. Jackson was suffering from a number of ailments such as lupus, arthritis, and vitiligo but was also addicted to drugs which he took to numb the pain he was suffering from due to these ailments. His personal physician, Dr. Conrad Murray, was convicted of involuntary manslaughter and served two years in prison after it was proven that his excessive administering of the drug was instrumental in his death. Michael Jackson was buried on February 3, 2010, after a truly private, public memorial service. Despite the negative part of his life, Michael Jackson will be sorely missed because his fans and many others believe that his major achievements outweigh his personal failings.

Health Issues

The Health Issues subsection addresses the health struggles that Michael Jackson faced in his final years, shedding light on the physical and emotional toll of these challenges. It offers a compassionate understanding of the complexities surrounding his health issues and their implications for his personal well-being and public image.

Health Issues Michael had always suffered from acne, but his skin had become much more severe since his 2005 trial. He was also diagnosed with vitiligo and lupus earlier, since 1986, which took its toll on him emotionally and physically. By 2009, he needed a lot of make-up to cover the patches of white skin left on his body, specifically on his chest and face. Vitiligo had consumed his skin, and under the pancake and spackle of cover-up, his face – what a terribly abused face – was almost white. However, lupus also left him with the added ordeal of blotching (or "blotches") of red and orange splotches. His dried-out, lupus-ed skin could not fully self-moisturize. When considering the grueling schedule of making albums or choreographing, and Michael's addiction to various narcotic painkillers, skin bleaching or lightening helped balance what the medicine and infirmity extracted by taking away the equality of Michael's acidic splotch of the colors his lupus added to what once was the glaring vitiligo snow of no melanin in his skin.

Michael confessed one of these to Black or White actor Macaulay Culkin in 1991, "overexposing" himself to the skin in the dermatologic effort to reach a lighter "blank canvas" for vitiligo dermatological corrective techniques, as Michael called the operative medical procedures that he took during dermatologic videotaped grainy camera session procedure distress he was enduring. He begged in vain for his equally narcissistic Broderick brothers to endure as entertaining "troopers" shoot others for Gregg Allman's suggested Circle Group filmed television show that Michael decided to do in 2001, as does then-Old Navy spokeslady Morgan Fairchild for her Old Navy adverts filming in 1998 to market in 1000 Dutched-up Big Lots, equally endorsing the obese overweight gals and slender Mr. Funs and Priced Depot discount "careerwear" work ensemble Mr. Men alike.

Death and Mourning

Since Jackson's passing, several lucrative ventures have been more or less built upon Jackson's back. Most of them have resulted in more interest in Jackson than before 2009. Most notably, Michael Jackson's This Is It netted over $260,000,000 in worldwide box office revenue alone in less than seven days.

Death and mourning

Amidst the frenzy caused from preparations for his series of 50 London concerts, the news of Jackson's sudden and unexpected death on June 25, 2009, was met by an uninterrupted global outpouring of grief, often accompanied by periods of reflection concerning the troubled aspects of his life. Supporters from all walks of life, often dissolving national and social boundaries, publicly mourned and privately contemplated what Jackson's now forty-five years of almost unceasing public life now meant. As it had been in his life, Jackson remained a repository for the feelings of others; as Diana Ross acted and generally has acted the part of the loving protector, Whitney Houston the part of the fragile and awkward dreamer, and Elton John the part of the waselike raconteur, Jackson had been the emblem, mnemonic or Rorschach visitation of our own childhoods and past wishes or, if not, of those things or experiences keeping us even now moored to life or living beyond it. L.A. fans previewing the movie Wild Hogs spontaneously honored the singer by standing up and giving a long ovation after the film in lieu of applause for flying crew.

Michael Jackson's death was a moment to remember and honor. TV shows were given over. Noticias (Spain) reported clutching her baby and openly crying, and Michael Jackson music played in every metro station as morning commuters listened. And a gold pool flotation toy bobbled regally south of Copacabana Beach with Michael Jackson's likeness painted over the float's head.

CHAPTER 8

Legacy and Cultural Impact

Michael Jackson's legacy as a global superstar has solidified over the years. His posthumous awards include, but are not limited to: the 2000s Artist of the Decade, the Recording Industry Association of America's Top Selling Artist of the Decade, and the Artist of the Century, World Music Awards' Best-Selling Pop and Best Selling Rock Artist of the Millennium, the Greatest Entertainer of All Time, 13 Grammy awards and the Grammy Lifetime Achievement award. He was inducted into the Rock and Roll Hall of Fame twice, and he is the first artist to have four top ten best-selling albums in the current year. After his death, his music sales worldwide increased 13 times over. He sold 35 million albums worldwide in total. Artists such as Justin Timberlake, Usher, Ne-yo, Robbie Williams, Chris Brown, Bruno Mars, Missy Elliot and many more have in some way taken inspiration for their music and dancing from Jackson. Jackson has been portrayed in movies such as his 1992 autobiography, The Jacksons: An American Dream, singing Michael Jackson: A Source of Inspiration 20 (from The Jacksons miniseries), The Wiz, Men in Black 2 and The Man in the Mirror: The Michael Jackson Story. He has been satirized in South Park, American Dad!,

Kappa Mikey and others. In 1988, he was immortalized as a robot in the Moonwalker video game for Sega. Many of these honors came after the lawsuit in 2005.

Headlines following Jackson's death underscored his place in American and global cultural life. For example, Variety ran a headline on June 25th, 2009 that read, "Michael Jackson dies at 50. The King of Pop's life, struggle to stage a comeback and sudden death." His impact on entertainment and popular culture cannot be understated. The MTV music video awards posthumously created an award category in Jackson's honor called "The Michael Jackson Video Vanguard Award," which in 2021 was renamed to the Michael Jackson Video Vanguard Encourage for Social Good, which went to Billie Eilish. It was won by Missy Elliot in 2019 and H.E.R. in 2020. In 2009, MTV designated September 18 as Michael Jackson Day and in 2011, he was recognized at the 53rd annual Grammy Awards with a 3D tribute. In 2012, PepsiCo and the Michael Jackson estate signed a contract for 30 years, valued between $10 and $15 million, for Jackson's likeness to be used for marketing purposes. Since 2011, Pepsi has given money to the Michael Jackson Diamond Celebration, which donates money to various Michael Jackson-related charities. The Reflection Section 21 of the Rock and Roll Hall of Fame, in 2012, created an exhibit which enshrined six Michael Jackson costumes from the 1980s. In 2008, his Thriller video was added to the National Film Registry, which selects films that are "culturally, historically, or aesthetically significant." Oprah Winfrey pre-recorded a final interview with Jackson in February 1993 and it aired in 2010. One significance of this is when Oprah began her show in 1986, she focused heavily on politics and the economy, but by the time she had Michael Jackson on her show in the early 1990s, Winfrey credited him with "saving my career." On February 24,

2019, again in 2020 and 2021, the pope declared his death to be the largest loss of the past decade.

Tributes and Honors

On August 1, 1972, Diana Ross introduced Michael Jackson and his brothers to the mayor of Gary, Indiana at the official dedication of the "Jackson Five Day" in Gary, Indiana. In December 1983, President Ronald Reagan presented Jackson with a Presidential Public Safety Communication Award in recognition of his support for the Ad Council's and the National Highway Traffic Safety Association's drunk driving prevention public service advertising programs. Jackson allowed the use of his song "Beat It" for the "Drinking and Driving Can Kill a Friendship" campaign.

Jackson's humanitarian work has received a number of awards. The singer is profiled in the "Public Service" area of the RFK Center website and named the 1984 "Man of the Year" by the Los Angeles chapter of the Civil Liberties Union. In 1984, he helped raise $250,000 to fight famine in Africa with UNICEF's "We Are The World" and was the American ambassador for the 39th World Assembly of the United Nations. On March 3, 1990, Jackson met with President George H.W. Bush's rolling "Win" Bush in the Oval Office. In August 2003, Jackson won the "Radio Music Award" for "Humanitarian of the Year" for his charity work, joining the United Negro College Fund and aiding in other benefits. In April 2006, audiences of the "Absolute Radio" network voted Michael number 5 of their "Perfect 10" - the biggest artists of all time. On September 26, 2006, Michael received the Diamond Award at the World Music Awards in London in recognition of his lifetime record sales.

CHAPTER 9

Conclusion

Michael Jackson was the greatest pop musician of all time. This essay has examined his life and the career highlights and setbacks that were interspersed within it. It has explored his iconic dance moves, his chart-breaking and atmospherically and emotionally powerful songwriting, his sheer worldwide appeal and humble nature, his finances and domestic relationships, his philanthropy, and his untimely death. It has identified the many conspiracy theories that blighted his name throughout his career, right up until he was well into his forties. It has acknowledged the legal disputes and scandals that marked his life, specifically between 1993 and 2005. It has separated the 'real' man (Michael Jackson, the shy and soft-spoken artist) from the 'faux' caricature (Michael Jackson, the camp but ruthless performer and fashion template) that the public and media construed him as.

In conclusion, irrespective of his shortcomings and eccentricities, we cannot deny the value and general importance of Michael Jackson's work and message. In his music, he spread messages of peace, hope, and love. He succeeded in his noble quest to achieve 'singing that means something', providing a cathartic experience to his listeners. He was transgressive too, recording songs about "Man in the Mirror" and being "Black or White" as he starred in "The Wiz" and thrilled the world in "Thriller"...selling out wherever he went. In that sense, Michael combined all of the knowledge he absorbed from other people and cultures as he journeyed through life, the arts, and the media from a young age. He was as good as the sum total of his parts. We can convince doubters by following Michael's life lesson: With a rightful and competitive presentation of your skills, knowledge, and passion, and despite the clowns and obstacles that will block you on the way, you're as good as the sum total of the instruction and experience you develop. Michael Jackson was the king of pop - so many raspy compilations sheet this access we naturally say - but he was also the king of being a real man who just happened to be an entertainer.

Reflections on Michael Jackson's Enduring Legacy

As time goes by, it becomes harder to imagine a world without Michael Jackson and his musical creations. His story has inspired fellowship and creativity among his followers and the broader population, echoing throughout several decades. Michael Jackson's story is more than that of a talented singer—he stands as an exponent of the indomitable artist consumed by an ungodly industry. Because of the ability of his character to point to a universal truth and serve as a rallying point for our efforts in this arena, Michael Jackson's story has become an insignium. It is for this reason that his story is so recurring. Every time people write or think about Michael Jackson, they think about the most pressing concerns facing them at the time. They connect Michael Jackson with the responses they themselves have been pursuing and with the thoughts they themselves have been developing. Michael Jackson is cherished not because he is ever locked in a fixed personality, but rather for his capacity to interact with others in a stable, more rounded connection which makes them feel pleasant, and in a place where they can understand, convey and clarify some of their thoughts, approaches, or faith.

The most far-reaching change we can make is to pause and think about the nature of Michael Jackson's inheritance. In order to approve of the quintessential Michael Jackson, one must consider both the origins of his schedule and of his creative exertions. He has excelled and exceeded by turning to a shared fascination with music, dance, praxis, and creativity. He reaches out to artisans aimed at identifying and highlighting someone worthy of reflection. In a culture in which these are two phenomena that are estranged from each other, stood the figure of Michael Jackson, who not only reconciled but also combined them. We should commemorate and analyze this element of Michael Jackson's special inheritance in a way that allows us to understand the secrets of his continuing sway; when we establish a connection with him, he becomes emblematic not as a ex repertoire seller but because of his talent for kindling prospects that work.